This Is NOT My Bed!

Written by
Jennifer Dupuis

Illustrated by
Carol Schwartz

For my sons Christopher and Jonathan who, much like this book, fill my heart with joy and keep me guessing with every turn of the page!
—JD

For my mom, who nurtured my artistic abilities from an early age.
—CS

Text Copyright © 2025 Jennifer Dupuis
Illustration Copyright © 2025 Carol Schwartz
Design Copyright © 2025 Tilbury House Publishers
Hardcover ISBN: 9781668955161

Library of Congress Cataloging Cataloging-in-Publication Data has been filed. LC record available at https://lccn.loc.gov/2025008523

Publisher expressly prohibits the use of this work in connection with the development of any software program, including, without limitation, training a machine learning or generative artificial intelligence (AI)system.

All rights reserved. No part of this book may be reproduced in any manner without the express written consent of the publisher, except in the case of brief excerpts in critical reviews and articles. All inquiries should be addressed to

TILBURY HOUSE PUBLISHERS

an imprint of
Cherry Lake Publishing Group
2395 South Huron Parkway, Suite 200
Ann Arbor, MI 48104
www.tilburyhouse.com

Printed in China

10 9 8 7 6 5 4 3 2 1

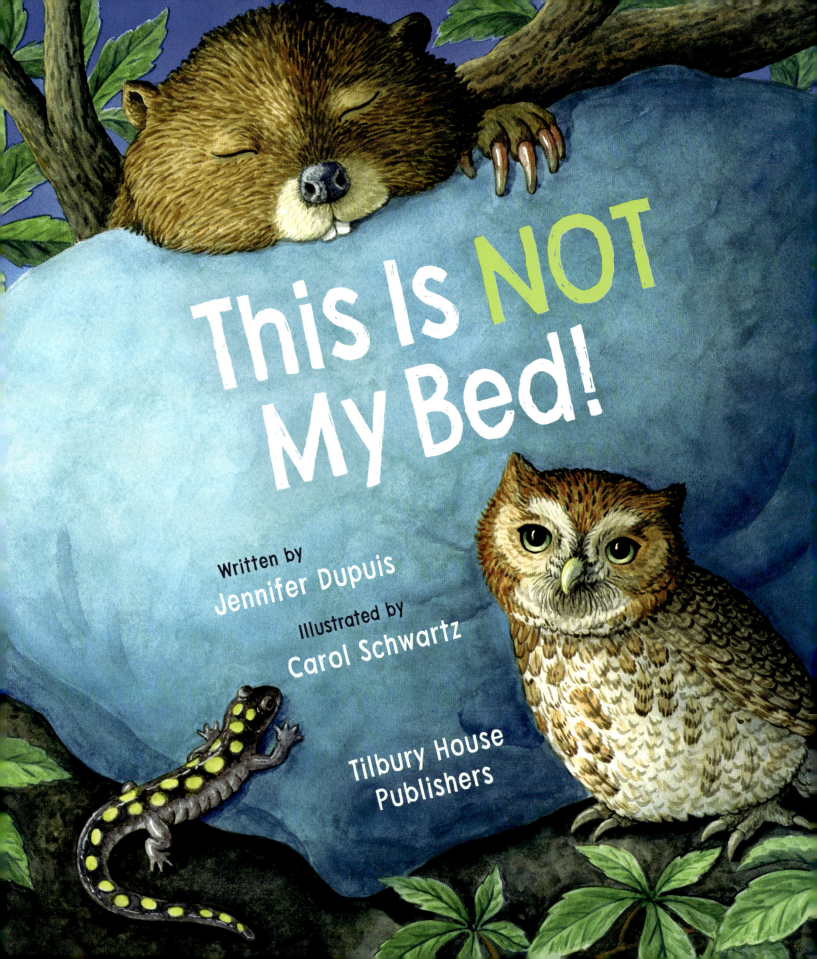

Good night. I'm ready—even though I'm not tired. *Y-a-aaa-awn*

I put on my pajamas.

I brushed my teeth.

I found my best buddy.

Time for bed. Here is my polka-dot pillow, but what is under my blanket?

Sharp sticks,

mushy mud,

loads of logs.

No, thank you! I will **NOT** sleep here! This is not my bed! This bed belongs to the . . .

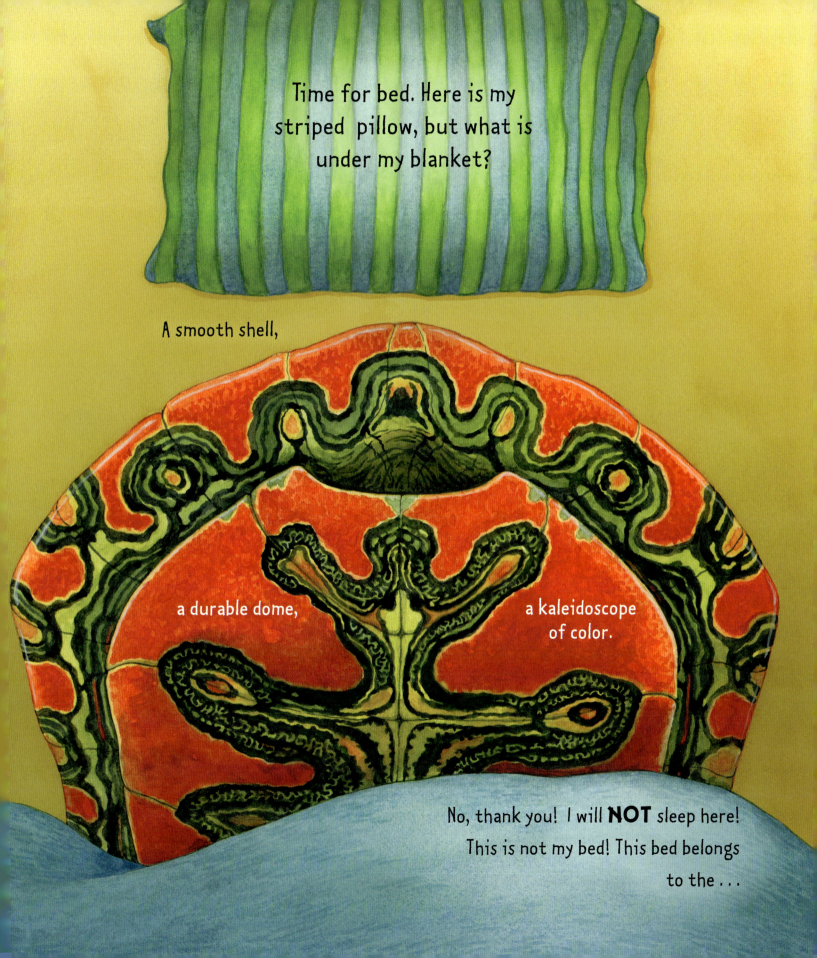

Time for bed. Here is my stinky pillow, but what is under my blanket?

A shimmering shallow,

a dark depth,

an aquatic abode.

No, thank you! I will **NOT** sleep here! This is not my bed! This bed belongs to the...

Time for bed. Here is my ruffly pillow, but what is under my blanket?

A secret place,

a high hollow,

a spot without sun.

No, thank you!
I will **NOT** sleep here!
This is not my bed!
This bed belongs to the...

Time for bed. Here is my swirly pillow, but what is under my blanket?

A tapestry of trees,

a cool clearing,

a patch of pine needles.

No, thank you! I will **NOT** sleep here! This is not my bed! This bed belongs to the . . .

Time for bed. Here is my soft pillow, but what is under my blanket?

A roof of rocks,

a span of soil,

a close-by creek.

No, thank you! I will **NOT** sleep here! This is not my bed! This bed belongs to the . . .

Time for bed. Here is my starry pillow, but what is under my blanket?

A quiet cave, a restful roost, plenty of pals to hang out with.

No, thank you! I will **NOT** sleep here! This is not my bed! This bed belongs to the...

LITTLE BROWN BAT

WHAT AM I?

Match each animal on the next page with its cozy bed!

What am I? I like . . .

1)   a colorful, protective shell.
2)   a hidden spot under the trees.
3)   braided branches and soft feathers.
4)   a dark, cool cave.
5)   sticks, mud, and logs.
6)   clear, fresh water.
7)   a hive.
8)   soft soil near a creek.
9)   a sleeping bag.
10)   a dark tree hollow.
11)   strands of sticky silk.
12)   an underground tunnel.

"It's surely our responsibility to do everything within our power to create
a planet that provides a home not just for us, but for all life on Earth."
—Sir David Attenborough, biologist, historian

ANSWER KEY 1:D, 2:G, 3:C, 4:J, 5:A, 6:E, 7:K, 8:H, 9:L, 10:F, 11:B, 12:I